W9-CAZ-042

DATE DUE

DEC 0 6 2001

GREAT EXPLORATIONS

FERDINAND MAGELLAN

First to Sail Around the World

MILTON MELTZER

BENCHMARK BOOKS

MARSHALL CAVENDISH
NEW YORK

With thanks to Professor David Armitage, Columbia University,
for his careful review of this manuscript.

Benchmark Books
99 White Plains Road
Tarrytown, New York 10591-9001
www.marshallcavendish.com

Library of Congress Cataloging-in-Publication Data
Meltzer, Milton, (date)
Ferdinand Magellan : first to sail around the world / by Milton Meltzer
p.   cm. – (Great explorations ; 1)
Includes bibliographical references and index (p.).
ISBN 0-7614-1238-7 (lib. Bdg.)
1. Magalhäes, Fernäo de, d. 1521—Journeys—Juvenile literature.
2.Explorers—Portugal—Biography—Juvenile literature. 3. Voyages around the world—Juvenile literature.
[1. Magellan, Ferdinand, d. 1521. 2. Explorers. 3. Voyages around the world.] I. Title. II. Series.
G286.M2 M46 2001   910'.92—dc21   [B]   00—064374

Photo Research by Candlepants Incorporated
Cover Photo: Giraudon / Art Resource, NY
The photographs in this book are used by permission and through the courtesy of: *Beinecke Rare Book and
Manuscript Library, Yale University*: 4, 41, 60, 67. CORBIS: 6. *Bettmann*: 8, 10. *Jim Sugar Photograph:*, 11.
Gianni Daglo Orti: 12, 20. *Nik Wheeler*: 55. *Michael Freeman*: 58. *Anthony Bannister-Gallo Images*: 65.
Owen Franken: 65 (inset). *Art Resource*, NY: *Giraudon*: 14, 17, 23, 35, 44, 48-49, 69. *Scala*: 28. *The Pierpont
Morgan Library:* 30-31. *Erich Lessing:* 19, 37, 72. *The Art Archive*: 24, 25, 27, 34, 52.
The New York Public Library, Astor, Lenox and Tilden Foundation: 63, 73.
Printed in Hong Kong
1   3   5   6   4   2

Contents

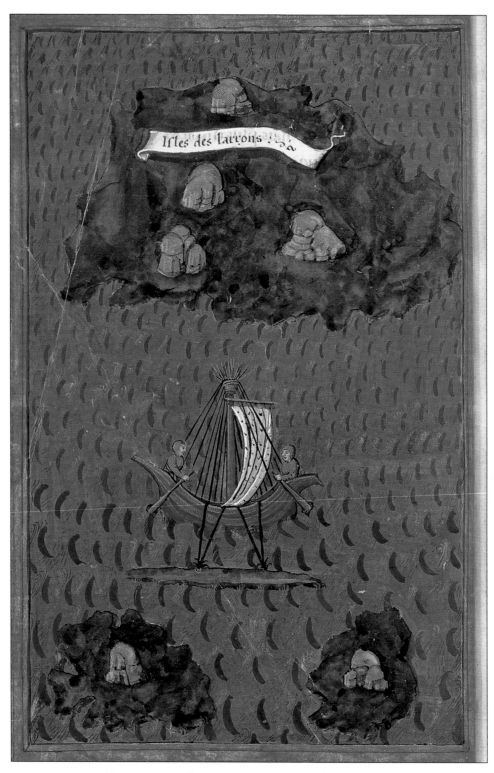

An illustration from Antonio Pigafetta's journal.

foreword

Can you imagine waking up one morning to learn that the earth had suddenly doubled in size? That was how stunned the people of Europe were when a battered old sailing ship staggered into a Spanish port, completing the first sea voyage around the world. The sailors brought news of a vast new ocean on the other side of the globe—the unimaginably big Pacific. The true measure of the earth's dimensions could now be taken. It was twice the size anyone had believed!

It was Ferdinand Magellan whose sailing ship completed the first circumnavigation of the globe in 1522—nearly five hundred years ago. To the map of the world he added the Pacific Ocean. You may have surfed the waves off a California beach, but you may not know that the Pacific occupies one-third of the earth's surface. Its area is greater than all the earth's land surfaces added together.

Magellan provided the first hard evidence that the world is round. Some thinkers had long believed that was so. He proved it. And proved too that all the seas are one. Think of the globe as an immense ball of water floating in space, in which the continents stand. If you look at a globe you'll see how true this is.

This book tries to give you some idea of what it was like to be alive in Magellan's time, what kind of man he was, and what the fantastic experience of that voyage around the world meant to him, to his sailors, and to people everywhere, then and now.

It is a story of one of the greatest heroes the world has known.

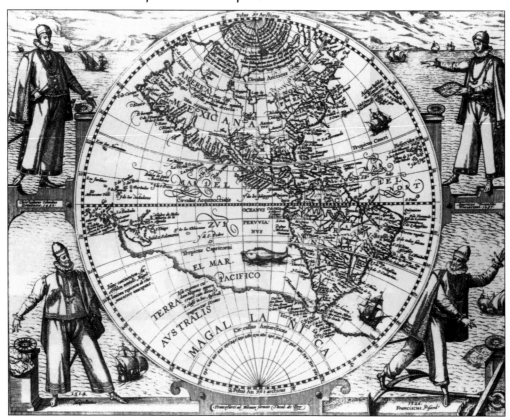

In this 1590 engraving by Flemish illustrator Theodore de Bry, four great explorers—(clockwise from top left) Christopher Columbus, Amerigo Vespucci, Ferdinand Magellan, and Francisco Pizarro—present a map of the Americas.

O N E

Mastering the Skills

We who are drowned every day in facts about and images of our world find it terribly hard to imagine ourselves living five centuries ago, in the time of Magellan. But let's try.

In 1450 most people never traveled farther than their town or village. Yet all around them were great civilizations they knew nothing of—in West Africa, in China and India, in Central and South America.

The fast travel and instant communication we take for granted did not exist in the fifteenth century. There were no planes, no televisions, no computers—few ways for people on different continents to know about one another. But by the 1450s, that had changed as a result of trade by land and sea. European seafarers, traders, and colonists had begun to explore—and exploit—the rest of the world. History began to

7

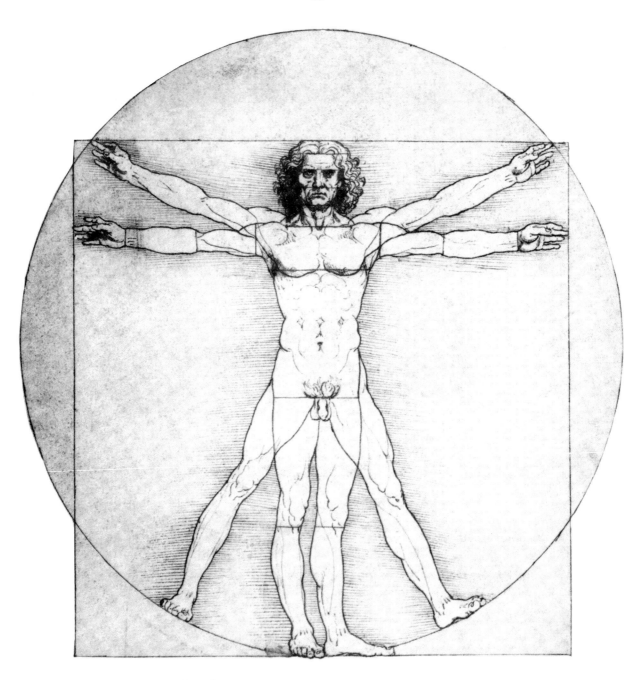

A study of man's proportions, drawn about 1490 by
Renaissance artist Leonardo da Vinci.

shift radically: from the story of this continent or that, to the story of one vast interconnected world.

Great advances took place in the arts and sciences. People began to think in new ways about the world and about their own place in it. The Renaissance (rebirth) is what this exciting period is called.

Magellan entered history on the dividing line between two worlds: the old one of the medieval era, or Middle Ages, which began around A.D. 450 with the breakup of the Roman Empire, and the new one of the Renaissance, the beginning of our modern age, which began in the 1400s. (You can't pinpoint the dates exactly, for social change overlaps and flows in many directions.)

The rigid beliefs of the Middle Ages had held people back from seeing new things, exploring new ideas. Even the best minds of the time were burdened with many superstitions.

But the coming of the Renaissance marked a great break with the past. Ancient manuscripts would be unearthed and scholarship revived. People felt a burning desire to rediscover and relearn what the ancient Greeks and Romans had known. Great universities would be founded. Cities would begin to grow. Architecture, painting, and sculpture would thrive. With the invention of movable type in the 1450s, printing presses would start to appear all over Europe. Mechanical clocks would come into wide use, changing people's thoughts about time. Improvements in the mariner's compass would allow sailors to navigate more surely. Columbus would reach the Americas. Magellan would sail around the world.

The Renaissance attitude was that human potential is unlimited. In this they broke with the mind-set of the Middle Ages—the belief that men and women are the helpless pawns of fate or Providence.

The home of the Renaissance was the Italian city of Florence, which produced many pioneers of the Renaissance: the painters Giotto and Masaccio, the architect Brunelleschi, the sculptors Ghiberti and Donatello,

Johann Gutenberg, the German inventor of a method of printing from movable type, shows a proof sheet to a patron.

and of course, Leonardo da Vinci: artist, scientist, architect, engineer, a man of boundless genius.

The term *humanism* is a label for the intellectual movement of the time. It signifies a fundamental shift from the God-centered world view of the Middle Ages to the human-centered view of the Renaissance. Humanists explored their relation to human society rather than to God.

In time, humanism reached into all branches of knowledge and art. It is credited with the concept of the human personality, the birth of history as the study of processes of change, and the principle of science that nothing should be taken as true unless it can be tried and demonstrated.

Yet a powerful belief in religion existed alongside the new faith in science. Christianity remained at the heart of European civilization.

A reconstructed astronomical telescope of Italian scientist Galileo in Florence, with the cathedral in the background. Florence was central to the Renaissance.

Magellan himself, a spearhead of exploration and discovery, was passionate about his religion's eternal truth. As we will see, he would go to the greatest lengths to convert to Christianity the peoples he encountered on his journey around the globe.

It seems odd that the man who discovered that the earth is twice as big as everyone thought it was came from a very small country. Ferdinand Magellan was born on a country estate in the north of Portugal between 1470 and 1480. (The precise date and place are not certain.) The climate in that mountainous district was hard. "Nine months of winter and three of hell," the locals said. Perhaps his growing up there shaped the tough character of the man he would become.

Magellan's was a noble family, tied distantly to royalty. At the age of

seven Ferdinand went to school at a nearby monastery. There he studied the catechism as well as reading, writing, arithmetic, and Latin. When he was about twelve his parents were able to place him as a page in the household of Queen Leonor, wife of King John II. There he had the company of an older brother, Diogo, who was then a senior page, and Francisco Serrano (possibly a cousin), who entered the court with Ferdinand. A friendship sprang up among the three that would continue throughout their lives.

In the palace, Ferdinand served as a messenger, usher, and attendant, even doing such domestic chores as making up the grand beds for visiting dignitaries. These tasks were meant to teach the young aristocrats disciplined service. The pages were taught far more, however. The king demanded that these boys be solidly trained in the maritime sciences that had become Portugal's key to success on the seas. For small as it was, Portugal was by now a great sea power. Magellan studied mapmaking, algebra, geometry, astronomy, and celestial navigation, taught by experienced navigators. The young pages were eager to hear the reports of voyagers returning from their missions abroad. What had they found? What wonders had they seen? What treasures had they brought home?

It became young Magellan's ambition to go to sea himself and win honor and glory for his own discoveries. That ambition was heated all the more when in March 1493 Christopher Columbus, returning from his first voyage, was driven into a Portuguese harbor by a storm at sea. The news of his arrival and his claim (mistaken) that his westward route had brought him to Asia electrified Portugal. King John, however, was less than thrilled, for had he not rejected Columbus's offer to make

The Iberian peninsula, in a fifteenth-century manuscript illumination taken from Ptolemy's Geography.

An artist's depiction of the departure of Christopher Columbus
from the port of Palos, Spain, on August 3, 1492.

that voyage under the flag of Portugal? Now Columbus had made his great discovery for Portugal's rival, Spain!

When his service as a page at court ended, Magellan stayed in Lisbon. He and his brother and cousin were given jobs at India House, the government agency for overseas trade, where the records of all maritime affairs were kept. Access to these was closely guarded, for the king's policy was to keep secret any information that might be of use to rivals.

But as an employee, Magellan was able to examine the globes, the maps, the ships' logs, and the reports of the explorers' discoveries. The king's science council was housed here too, and Magellan listened in on discussions of new geographic concepts and navigational theories. India House helped to outfit the ships leaving for India each year. From the pilots and masters who made those voyages Magellan picked up many practical aspects of navigation: rigging, caulking, repairing ships, placing armaments aboard, procuring and loading supplies for the long, long voyages—what didn't he learn of them? The skills he mastered only intensified his passion to sail on one of those splendid voyages into the unknown.

Getting His Chance

The great voyages at the dawn of the Age of Discovery were carried out mostly by the adventurous Portuguese and Spaniards. The first to inspire these ventures was Prince Henry of Portugal (1394-1460). Later he would be called Henry the Navigator, not because he went to sea himself, but because he encouraged exploration. He supplied the ships, the money, and the organization required.

It's hard for us to grasp how little the Europeans of Henry's time knew of the world beyond their borders. To the south and east of Europe lay a crescent of Muslim states barring the paths to the rest of Africa and to China. To the west was the Atlantic Ocean, which both Christians and Muslims considered uncrossable. In 1400 the products traded to Europe came from the Muslim East or across the Mediterranean from Muslim Africa, and the bulk of that trade was controlled

Henry the Navigator is portrayed in this detail from a painting in the National Museum of Art in Lisbon, Portugal.

by the merchants of Genoa, Venice, and other Italian ports. Though Portuguese merchants were doing well dealing in wine, fish, and salt, they saw fatter profits to be had from gold, spices, and sugar. But how were they to grab a slice of that business? The Italian city-states were protected by strong naval forces and old ties with the East.

As a young man of twenty-one, Prince Henry took part in the 1415 campaign to take Ceuta, a town on the North African coast of the Mediterranean, opposite Gibraltar. Ceuta was a terminus for caravans bringing gold and other valuable goods across the Sahara into the markets of Morocco. The Portuguese saw it as the gateway to new sources of gold and spices, and when they captured Ceuta, they proved that winning new lands and new trading centers was not as difficult or as risky as they had feared.

Henry wanted to learn a lot more about Africa. In 1416 he built a naval arsenal at Sagres on Cape Saint Vincent, the southernmost promontory of Portugal. He used this site as a center for geographical and astronomical records, making it a base for exploration. Until then, the Portuguese knew only the nearby coastline of the Atlantic, and nothing of its huge reach north and south from the Arctic to the Antarctic, nor east and west from the continents of Europe and Africa to the then unknown continents of North and South America.

Prince Henry's experts brought several innovations to the science of navigation. Among them were the wind-rose compass, the crude forerunner of the modern mariner's compass; the astrolabe, which helped pilots find their bearings when far from land; and a great improvement in sailing ships, the caravel. Caravels had much greater ability to make use of varying winds than the bigger, heavier merchant ships called carracks, and were vastly superior in maneuverability and speed.

The men Henry sent to sea began to inch their way southward, down the western coast of Africa. In 1444, one of his captains, Gil Eannes, brought two hundred black slaves into Portugal, which opened

An astrolabe, used in Poland around 1500. The circumference of the metal disk is marked off in degrees.

up the terrible European slave trade that would last for more than four hundred years. Though Henry died in 1460, the exploration went on, now in the hope of finding a sea route to the Indies and their spices and gold. In 1488 Bartholmeu Dias rounded the Cape of Good Hope at the southern tip of Africa. A decade later Vasco da Gama pioneered the route to Calicut in India. By 1513 the first Portuguese ship had reached Canton in China.

THE QUARRY WAS SPICES

The desire for spices changed history. It arose in part from the monotony of the diet in the Middle Ages, and from the lack of means of preserving food, especially meat.

Spices—pepper, cinnamon, cloves, nutmeg, ginger, saffron, and a host of others—all came from the Far East, chiefly from the Molucca, or Spice, Islands. The Moluccas lay toward the eastern end of a scattered archipelago of 13,000 islands (now part of Indonesia). Europeans' dreams of paradise were permeated with the smell and taste of spices. The Spice Islands, the place where they grew, became the center of international and often deadly competition, and the source of great fortunes. A spice that had cost one ducat in the Moluccas could sell in Western Europe for one hundred times as much.

By the fifteenth century, spices and oriental luxury goods had become so valuable that several European powers were casting about for ways to gain control of the products. What drove Columbus, Magellan, and others to risk their ships and their lives? The search for a westward passage to the land of spices.

A nutmeg merchant of the fifteenth century, shown in a manuscript illumination.

Getting His Chance

When forty-year-old Vasco da Gama returned to Portugal in 1499 with a cargo of spices, the profit from his voyage whetted young Magellan's appetite for making his own fortune. Early the next year, as another expedition was being fitted out for India, Magellan tried to sign up. But it took political influence to be allowed to enlist, and the obscure India House clerk was denied. Several years passed before he finally got his chance. In 1505, Ferdinand, Diogo, and Francisco, the three friends who had shared a dozen years of training at India House, were assigned to the command of Francisco de Almeida, the appointed viceroy of India. His instructions were to establish fortified trading posts and naval bases on the east coast of Africa and the west coast of India. But his true intent was to take over the entire spice route and the spice sources themselves.

T H R E E

Trade and Trouble

It was a big fleet that sailed for the Indian Ocean—22 ships, carrying 1,500 soldiers, 200 artillerymen, and 400 "gentlemen adventurers," including Magellan. These supernumeraries, or "supers"—men who served without pay—were to carry out any military or civil duties assigned them. Committed to three years' service, every man in the fleet knew he might never return. The death rate from previous expeditions was enormous. Men died of battle wounds, disasters at sea, scurvy, cholera, and tropical diseases.

Magellan carried aboard ship a sea chest for his belongings, including his arms and a suit of armor. He, Diogo, and Francisco, as supers, stowed their chests and weapons, lashed down, in a corner of the open deck. Magellan slept on the open deck, with no shelter from weather and no privacy. A blanket roll was his bedding. There were only two enclosed privies jutting out at the back of each ship, which emptied into the sea. In rough weather you couldn't get to a privy. The result was an intolerable stink and swarms of rats and cockroaches. Only the ship's captain and the high officers had cabins.

All men aboard had the same rations: tough salted beef or pork for the main meal; rice, cheese, or salt fish; claret and water once daily. There were no cooks on board, and food was usually eaten cold, for no fires were allowed on account of the frequent windy weather.

Sailing down the coast of Africa the fleet experienced storms and

Ships departing from Lisbon in the 1500s,
in an engraving by Theodore de Bry.

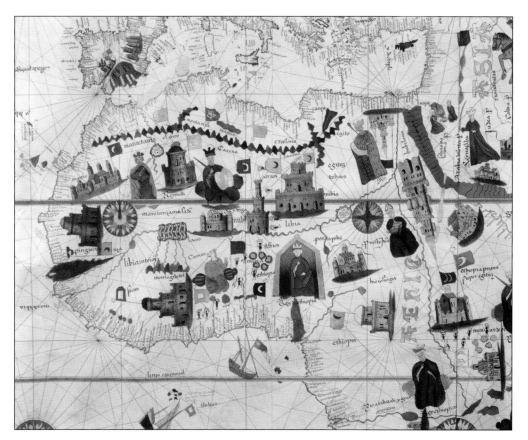

The Mediterranean and North Africa, a detail from
a world map of 1500 made by Juan de la Cosa.

calms and periods of despair as the pilots groped blindly through unknown hazards. Three months after leaving Lisbon, they rounded the Cape of Good Hope. Then they headed north-northeast and after losing some sailors washed overboard in heavy weather, entered the calmer waters of the Indian Ocean.

Their plan was to take over the spice sources and routes, but without a large military force, they had to count on superior naval power to overcome opposition. The Portuguese would soon gain a reputation for utter ruthlessness. Again and again, Almeida deposed hostile local

An atlas of the mid-1500s shows part of the east coast
of Africa and the Indian Ocean.

leaders, replacing them with friendlier rivals who swore loyalty to the Portuguese king. He built forts and left behind military units to defend them. At Mombasa, he sacked and torched the city to punish a sheik who resisted being taken over.

That fall of 1505, part of the fleet left for Portugal with a cargo of spices and other merchandise. The ruler of Calicut and his Egyptian allies plotted a surprise attack on the remaining ships. Told of the plot by an informer, the Portuguese routed the attacking fleet. It was here that Magellan probably received the first of many wounds he would suffer during these years abroad.

Magellan's whereabouts during the next year or two are impossible to trace. But in December 1508, Almeida, whose son had been killed in a sea battle, set out to avenge that loss by tracking down the Egyptian-Indian squadron he blamed for it. He found the enemy in a harbor, bombarded the fortress protecting it, and when it was crushed, let loose his troops to savage the city. They spared no one: even women and children were murdered.

Six weeks later, Almeida caught up with another enemy armada and hammered it mercilessly. Magellan was wounded again in the hand-to-hand fighting. The bloody-minded Almeida then ordered the Venetian gunners on the captured Egyptian ships to be tortured. Their agony ended only when their broken bodies were tied to the mouths of cannon and blown to bits.

That naval victory gave the Portuguese control of the sea routes between India and Europe, ending Venetian domination of the European spice trade.

When Magellan recovered from his wounds, he joined a flotilla ordered to seize and establish a base at Malacca, on the southwest coast of the Malay Peninsula near modern Singapore. Malacca was the most prized port on the spice route across Asia to the West. The valuable products of the Orient—cloves, cinnamon, nutmeg, mace, pepper, gold,

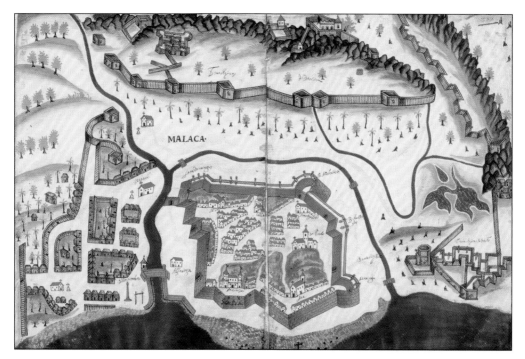

Malacca, around 1511, part of the Malay Peninsula
and an important hub of the Spice Islands.

porcelains, silks, drugs—passed through the city en route to Europe. Arab and Chinese merchants had controlled this port for centuries.

That expedition failed, but three years later, in 1511, another attempt to seize Malacca succeeded. This time the Portuguese had a more powerful fleet, superior weapons, and troops hardened by many campaigns. The invaders wished to do as little damage as possible to the city because of the treasures it held. But they showed no mercy for the people. As the troops moved through the streets, they cut down men, women, and children who tried to flee. Those who surrendered were enslaved. From these captives Magellan acquired a young Malay slave to whom he gave the name Enrique de Malacca.

The sacking of Malacca brought the greatest spoils of war ever taken by the Portuguese. The enormous plunder, held for the king and

A Strange Treaty

After Columbus blundered upon the Americas, the European powers quickly grasped the possibilities of colonizing vast new regions. The chief competitors were Spain and Portugal, at that time the leading maritime nations. When King John of Portugal got word of what Columbus had found, he announced that these new lands belonged to his country. The claim was disputed by the King of Spain.

Both rulers looked to the pope, Alexander VI, to settle their disagreement. The pope had the power to assign to Catholic kings the government of all newly discovered parts of the earth.

The result was the Treaty of Tordesillas (1494), one of the strangest diplomatic agreements in history. The pope drew a theoretical line dividing the world into two halves, giving Portugal the Eastern Hemisphere and Spain the Western. The imaginary line of demarcation was drawn from pole to pole.

Because longitudinal measurement was inexact at that time, each nation claimed that the Moluccas, the Spice Islands, lay within its boundary. Both sides refused to concede anything, and the matter wouldn't be settled until the mid-sixteenth century.

Pope Alexander VI, who divided the world between Portugal and Spain, in a detail from a painting by Pinturicchio.

the captains of the fleet, was shipped to the port of Goa in India. On the way, the ship struck a reef in a storm and sank, with most of the sailors and all the treasure lost.

Magellan was placed on patrol duty, in command of a ship, and saw more action in several raids upon nearby pirate strongholds. Francisco Serrano, while on another expedition, wound up in Ternate, one of the most important spice islands. There the rajah gave him command of his armed forces. He acted as peacemaker among Moslem groups and soon married the daughter of the ruler of the neighboring island of Tidore. From here he sent frequent letters to Magellan telling how easy it was to become rich on these islands and urging him to join him.

Those letters, and his own experience, made Magellan certain that he could reach the Spice Islands more easily by sailing west than by the long, difficult voyage around the Cape of Good Hope. But to go that route, he knew he had to find a strait through Spanish America. And he believed he knew where he could find one.

For by this time some twenty years had passed since Columbus's first voyage to the New World. Other explorers too had reached the Americas, and mapmakers were sketching in the outlines of these continents. But no one yet had any idea how vast the ocean west of the Americas was. Magellan must have thought—mistakenly—that the Spice Islands would be within easy sailing distance once he got past Spanish America.

Now a veteran sailor and soldier, Magellan returned to Portugal around 1512. The next year, he was summoned to serve in the cavalry force of an expedition against the Moroccan town of Azamor, which had rebelled against paying annual tribute to its Portuguese overlords. The town surrendered quickly, but desert troops outside continued to resist. Fighting against them, Magellan suffered a personal disaster. An enemy lance pierced his knee, leaving him partially crippled. For the rest of his life he would walk with a limp.

The fleet of Pedro Alvares Cabral, the Portuguese navigator who on his way to India claimed the discovery of Brazil.

Even worse troubles awaited him. On returning to Lisbon he was accused of trading with the enemy, of putting into his own pocket money from the sale of captured cattle. Magellan protested his innocence to Portugal's ruler, King Manuel, and asked for a small raise in his military pay. The king doubted his innocence and refused the raise. Was his devotion to the crown, his suffering and sacrifice of no account? Were this pampered king and court indifferent to a man who had helped to build Portugal's power and fame?

After several years of service, no longer a young man, with no influence in high places, Magellan seemed to face a bleak future.

f O U R

Voyage into the Unknown

Despite his rejection, two years later, in 1516, Magellan made another appeal to King Manuel. He asked to be given command of an expedition to the Moluccas. There, as an agent of the crown, he would help his friend Serrano establish a strong and profitable Portuguese trading center. No doubt he did not mention sailing westward to get there, for that would have taken him through Spanish territory. And Spain would have profited, not Portugal. No, he would take instead the route around the Cape of Good Hope.

He used Serrano's glowing account of the wealth to be derived from the spices in the islands to tempt the King. But Manuel would have none of it. He still distrusted Magellan and refused his request, dismissing him rudely. When Magellan knelt to kiss the king's hand, Manuel disdainfully withheld it. Go where you like, he shouted, I don't care what you do!

Charles V, king of Spain and Holy Roman Emperor, as painted by Italian artist Titian.

Humiliated before the court, Magellan left Lisbon, renouncing his Portuguese citizenship. He took his appeal to Spain's monarch, young King Charles, soon to be Emperor Charles V of the Holy Roman Empire. But before leaving Portugal, Magellan collected all the information he could from friendly Portuguese pilots and their maps, charts, and globes.

The port of Seville, a detail from a painting
by Alonso Sanchez Coello.

In the fall of 1517 he arrived in Seville, now the center of Spain's trade with the Americas. Soon afterward he met the influential Diogo Barbosa, married his daughter Beatriz, and received a handsome dowry. (She would bear him a son and conceive a second child before his departure.) It took months for Magellan to convince young King Charles and his advisors that he was a reliable and competent man for the voyage he was promising.

What was Magellan like at this time? In his early forties, probably, he was short but powerfully built, dark-complexioned, black-bearded, and above all, tough. Magellan had influential friends who told the king of his courage and decisiveness fighting in the Far East, his dedication to the cause of Christ and eagerness to spread the Gospel, his intimate knowledge of the Orient, and his belief that he could reach Asia by going through a strait at the foot of South America.

Magellan showed the king a globe that indicated the Spice Islands lay in the Spanish part of the world and not too far from the west coast of America. No one had any idea how wide the Pacific is, for no European had yet crossed it.

The teenaged king, thrilled to be patron of a daring voyage into the unknown, approved Magellan's plan. In March 1518 he appointed Magellan captain general and commander of the fleet, and allotted him 10 percent of any profit made from the expedition, as well as noble titles his children could inherit and other privileges.

When more funding than the king could supply was needed, foreign investors stepped in. For the next year-and-a-half Magellan set about finding ships and arranging for provisions for a voyage that might last two years. He needed trade goods that would be acceptable to many people he might do business with.

And, of course, he had to recruit crews. This proved troublesome, for many sailors feared such unpredictable and risky voyages. He tried to enlist experienced Portuguese veterans of Asian voyages, but the

The <u>Victoria</u>, one of the five ships Magellan commanded
on his first westward voyage around the world.

Spanish authorities resisted, forcing him to replace most of the officers with Spaniards. The seamen, promised an annual wage, were given four month's pay in advance.

By the time of sailing Magellan had supreme command of five ships: his flagship, the *Trinidad*, and the *San Antonio*, the *Concepcion*, the *Victoria*, and the *Santiago*. They were all merchant ships called carracks except for the *Santiago*, which was a caravel, the best he could get with his the limited funds. They carried relatively heavy armaments, with eighty-two mounted guns and a supply of small arms, crossbows, picks, and body armor.

The ships' crews totaled about 270 men of many different nationalities—Spanish, Portuguese, Italian, Flemish, English, German, Irish, Malaysian, and a few blacks. Magellan knew there would be trouble ahead managing so motley a crew. The Spanish and the Portuguese were deeply prejudiced against each other. He heard rumors that King Manuel of Portugal, calling him a traitor for serving Spain, was conspiring with the Portuguese officers to sabotage the voyage. One of King Charles's chief councilors, the Spanish bishop, Fonseca, was furious that he had given the command of a Spanish naval fleet, and sweeping powers in the new lands they were expected to discover, to a Portuguese. To undermine Magellan's authority, Fonseca had placed his own agents in command of three of Magellan's five ships.

At last, on September 20, 1519, the fleet weighed anchor and sailed into the Atlantic. Disaster and death lay ahead.

And everlasting fame.

Magellan's Voyage
1518–1522

PACIFIC OCEAN

GUAM

PACIFIC OCEAN

NORTH AMERICA

ARCTIC

ASIA

SPAIN
PORTUGAL
Strait of Gibraltar
Cape Verde

EGYPT
AFRICA

INDIA

PHILIPPINES

THE MOLUCCAS
(Spice Islands)

ATLANTIC

OCEAN

BRAZIL

INDIAN

OCEAN

SOUTH AMERICA

Cape of Good Hope

PATAGONIA

Strait of Magellan

ANTARCTICA

AUSTRALIA

FIVE

Mutiny, Starvation, Disease

One of the most important foreigners aboard the flagship as the voyage began was an Italian volunteer, Antonio Pigafetta. About 30, he came from a prominent family of Vincenza. While serving with the papal ambassador to the court of King Charles, he learned of Magellan's project. Excited by the prospect of seeing "with my own eyes" unknown parts of the world, he arranged to be sent along as a Vatican observer.

Pigafetta kept a richly detailed diary, making entries every day. He managed, sometimes by signs, more often through Magellan's slave, the Malay interpreter Enrique, or in direct if halting conversation, to learn what the people they encountered thought or wanted. He had a lively interest in them and absorbed a great amount of information on their daily life, weapons, housing, food, faith, trade and barter, even relations with other people or kingdoms. He noted the flora and fauna wher-

Prologue de Anthoine Pigaphete sur le present liure sien
traictant La nauigation des isles de Maluque: fernand de Maga,
glianes Portugaloys capitaine general de larmee voyagiere: Et la
hayne que les patrons et aultres capitaines auoient contre luy

Chapitre - Premier :

Ource quily a plusieurs gentz curieux (tres
illustre et tres reuerend Seigneur) qui non
seullement se contentent descoutter et scauoir
les grandes et merueilleuses choses que dieu
ma permys veoir et souffrir en la longue et perilleuse nauigation
que iay faicte cy apres escripte. Mais ancores veullent scauoir les
moyens et facons: et le chemin que iay tenu pour y aller, non ad,
ioustant foy ny ferme creance a la fin si premierement ilz ne sont
bien aduertiz et cerciorez du commancement. Pourtant
Monseigneur il vous plaira entendre que me trouuant en
Espaigne lan de la natiuite nostre seigneur Mil cinq centz dix et
neuf a la court de serenissime roy des Rommains auecq le reuered
seigneur Mons.r Francoys Cheregato alors prothonotaire apos,
tolique et ambassadeur du pape Leon dixiesme: Le quel par
sa vertu peruint depuys a leuesche de Aprutino et principaulte
de Theramo: Et congnoissant tant par lecture de plusieurs
liures que par rapport de plusieurs clercz et entenduz qui d
practiquoyent auecq ledit prothonotaire les tresgrandes et
espouentables choses de la mer occean/ie deliberay (auecq la
bonne grace de lempereur et du susdit seigneur) experimenter
et aller veoir a loeil partie desdictes choses: Au moyen de

Entreprise de Anthom
Pigaphete de la nauig
tion de la superieure
Inde:

A page from the first chapter of a printed edition
of Pigafetta's journal, the only written account of
Magellan's voyage.

ever they went and built vocabularies of words spoken by each of the people they encountered. He tended to believe fantastic tales told to him, but nevertheless his journal is the most complete record of the expedition and will be quoted here often.

Magellan gave the fleet's officers strict rules designed to keep the ships together and under his control. Sailing southward along the African coast, they soon reached the Canary Islands, where they loaded on water, wood, fresh meat, and salted codfish. As they were about to leave, a ship brought Magellan warning from his father-in-law that the three Spanish captains, Bishop Fonseca's men—Cartagena, Mendoza and Queseda—were planning to kill him. Magellan sent back word not to worry, he would do whatever was necessary to carry out his mission.

As the fleet prepares to sail, let's stop for a moment to think of what Magellan did not have to help his crews on their way:

- No accurate map
- No accurate compass
- No accurate clock
- No weather forecasting source
- No knowledge of how to figure out longitude—that is,
  to know precisely where the ships were
- No radio to communicate with shore or other ships at sea in case
  of emergency
- No source of power to propel the ships except for wind and oars

Leaving the Canaries, they passed by the Cape Verde islands and continued to sail along the African coast down to Sierra Leone. It was the route Portuguese pilots believed best to take before crossing west to Brazil. But the three Spanish captains challenged Magellan's judgment in sailing so far south. When Cartagena tried to get other officers behind him, Magellan had him arrested and put in irons, stifling this first attempt at mutiny.

Ten weeks after leaving Spain, the fleet was off the coast of Brazil. Rather than land where the Portuguese had long been trading, Magellan sailed farther south. On December 13, 1519, he cast anchor at what is now the harbor of Rio de Janeiro. The sailors, exhausted and hungry for fresh food, went ashore to find a "plentiful refreshment" of "the most delicious fruits" and llama meat. And, Pigafetta adds, Indian maidens, beautiful and welcoming.

The natives had never before seen white men or ships. Because it rained the day Magellan arrived, the people believed that these were men from the skies who had come to break the two-month drought. Pigafetta wrote, "They thought that the small boats of the ships were the children of the ships, and that the said ships gave birth to them when the boats were lowered to send the men hither and yon. And when the boats were lying alongside a ship, they thought that the ships were suckling them."

After thirteen days in port, the fleet continued to move southward in search of a strait to the Pacific. The ships tried to stay close to shore. But often storms and sudden squalls would nearly wreck them. One storm drove them all out to sea, and for frightening hours they lost sight of one another. Another time some sailors landed on an islet to kill seals and penguins for fresh meat, but a storm prevented them from getting back to the ship. They had to burrow under the mound of carcasses to keep from freezing to death.

Magellan's flagship was always out front, piloting the course over uncharted seas, around headlands, into bays, past sand banks and hidden reefs. The strain must have come near breaking even this tough leader. For some sixty days he never had rest or warm dry clothing. Riggings were coated with ice and decks awash in mountainous green seas. Hail and sleet ripped into every corner of the ships. No fire could be lighted, so no warm food could be had. The sailors' soaked clothes froze so solid they crackled when they moved. The salt water in them

Crew members scramble aboard after chopping a narrow passage
through Antarctic ice in this engraving by Theodore de Bry.

caused skin to chafe and sores to erupt, palms and fingers to crack, and
fingernails to fall off. The tips of ears, noses, and toes were frostbitten.

Their next landing was on the bleak coast of Patagonia, a desolate
place where only a handful of people lived. Here the major task of exploration would begin, for this region was totally unknown to Europeans.
And it was here that Magellan faced a great crisis. The fleet put in at
what is now Port San Julian, to wait out the winter. It was late March
1520. Great storms and freezing cold made this Antarctic region almost

unbearable. The sea was too rough for ships to penetrate further into unknown waters.

Did this Portuguese outsider know what he was doing? the aristocratic Spanish captains asked. He had treated them with little respect (their knowledge of the sea was nonexistent) and was causing the fleet to rove blindly and endlessly over the ocean in search of a strait he didn't even know existed. This was their excuse to carry out what they had plotted before leaving Spain. They would arrest Magellan, carry him home in chains, and prove to King Charles that he had gambled on a man who was an outright fraud.

Magellan suspected a revolt was brewing. He decided to force the captains to show their hand. He summoned all officers and pilots to dine with him after mass on Palm Sunday. Only Mesquita, a Portuguese officer, showed up. A deliberate insult by the others! That night Cartagena's group took over the *San Antonio*. Now the rebels controlled three ships of the fleet.

Never one to panic, Magellan took a daring step. The mutineers had asked for a meeting with him, promising obedience to his orders if they could reach an agreement. Guessing that this was a ruse to capture him, Magellan sent seven men to their ship, the *Victoria*, with a letter to the captain, Mendoza. Magellan's loyal men came aboard, with weapons concealed in their clothing. While Mendoza was reading Magellan's message, one man stabbed him in the throat, while a second crushed his skull. Then another boatload of loyal men sent by Magellan clambered aboard and took over the *Victoria*.

With three loyal ships, Magellan was able to block exit from the harbor. When the *San Antonio* tried to escape in the night, Magellan's men grappled with it and forced it to surrender. Only the *Concepcion* was still in the hands of mutineers. But alone and helpless, its captain, Cartagena, surrendered.

The mutineers—officers and the men who joined them—had to be punished. A court martial was held, with all evidence recorded. Captain Mendoza had already been killed aboard the *Victoria*, but by custom his body was hanged, drawn, and quartered. The court pronounced Quesada a traitor too and had him beheaded. Magellan hesitated to execute the condemned third officer, Cartagena, perhaps because of his closeness to his powerful sponsor, Bishop Fonseca. Instead, Cartagena was sentenced to be marooned on the grim shore of Patagonia. (Nothing was ever heard of him again.)

Although some forty other mutineers were sentenced to death, Magellan, realizing he needed their manpower, commuted their sentences to hard labor.

As captain general of the fleet, Magellan had always stood somewhat apart from his subordinates. But now, after the turmoil of the mutinies, there were none close to him except for his page and his slave, Enrique de Malacca. In his isolation, Magellan, who had always been devoutly religious, began to develop a belief that he had been chosen by God for this mission. He felt certain that he would never lack divine protection.

For five months the fleet dared not venture beyond San Julian. Meanwhile the ships were careened—that is, pushed over to one side so that their bottoms could be scraped, seams caulked, and braces strengthened. While this work was being done, Magellan had the *Santiago*, captained by Juan Serrano, inch its way southward in search of the strait he was betting on. Sixteen days later Serrano came upon a protected bay he called Santa Cruz. But as he sailed out to sea again, his ship foundered. He managed to beach it on a sandbank, but it was sucked off the beach, broke up, and disappeared with all its gear and cargo.

Would Serrano and his crew starve there in the piercing cold? Two sailors offered to trudge overland back to San Julian to get help. By some miracle, after eleven days they managed to make it, so emaciated that at first they were not recognized. Magellan sent a rescue ship to bring the others back safely. All thirty-seven members of the crew but one survived.

Magellan and his men thought no one lived in this territory, until one day they encountered a Patagonian. He made real the ancient legend of a race of giants. "So tall was this man," reported Pigafetta, "that we came up to the level of his waistbelt. He had a broad face, painted red. His hair was short and colored white, and he was dressed in skins." He was a big fellow, no doubt, perhaps six-and-a-half feet tall, but because Magellan was short, as were many of his men, he probably seemed much bigger

On Serrano's advice, Magellan moved the fleet to the better anchorage at Santa Cruz. Two months more passed with the men hunting, fishing, and trapping in a desperate effort to keep from starving. For with winter at hand, Magellan realized he had been criminally cheated by the suppliers in Seville. They had been paid to provision the fleet for a two-year voyage, but had faked the records and put aboard only half the needed amount. (Apparently such corruption was not uncommon, and veterans like Magellan tried to guard against it. But the thieving suppliers resorted to dozens of tricks and deceptions to escape detection.)

So the hunt for food was a life or death necessity. Magellan had to get enough to sustain his crews on the voyage across the Pacific—if, that is, they could find the strait.

As spring came on, the ships again set sail on their search for a passage to the Pacific. They sailed four days beyond Santa Cruz until they saw an opening like a bay. Everyone must have prayed that this time the bay would open to the precious strait. But how could it? For it seemed closed on all sides. The crew was remembering the Strait of Gibraltar, a simple open passage connecting the Mediterranean with the Atlantic, which you could see through. But Magellan was not.

Maybe, Pigafetta wrote, he had seen a secret map in Portugal that showed a far different kind of strait, a well-hidden one.

Well-hidden? Worse than that! The Strait of Magellan, as it was later named, proved to be "the narrowest, most devious, most circuitous of all the straits connecting two great bodies of water." It is a tortuous passage, littered with small islands and unexpected patches of water. On the Atlantic side are low grassy banks, but on the Pacific side the strait is a fjord between towering, craggy, ice-capped mountains.

A sixteenth-century map shows part of the Strait of Magellan.

Wisely, Magellan did not risk all four ships at once. He sent the biggest, the *San Antonio*, ahead to check one possible opening, but it proved to be a dead end. That ship's pilot, Esteban Gomes, who hated Magellan because he had not appointed him captain, mutinied while out of sight of the fleet, clapped the captain in irons, turned the ship around, and piloted it back to Spain. All this was unknown to Magellan, who would not live to learn what happened to it.

Now the three remaining ships kept together as they searched for

as traversed later by the fleet of Admiral George Spilbergen.

a view of the open sea. Up this passage and that, back and forth, in and out, only to be sadly disappointed time and again by countless misleading bays and rivers. Never quitting, Magellan sensed one day that the end of the strait was close. He sent a boat ahead to probe. Three days later the sailors returned to report that they had rounded a cape and seen the sea, the open sea! Then Magellan "wept for joy," Pigafetta noted, "and called that cape Cape Desire, for he had been desiring it for a long time."

It took thirty-eight days for Magellan's ships to maneuver the 334 miles between the two oceans. You may imagine what courage it took to defy the elements and hold the crews together on this first passage through the strait. In times to come other ships would attempt it, and simply quit.

Where was Magellan now? How big was this vast watery emptiness ahead of him? How long would it take to sail across it? All those who had previously estimated its size were at least 80 percent short of its actual extent.

When Magellan found out how big the Pacific really was, it came as an agonizing surprise.

SIX

Across the Pacific

When Magellan entered the Pacific he was in unknown waters. He had no notion that it covers one-third of the total area of the globe. How could he have known? In whatever maps he may have seen before the voyage, the "South Sea," as it was called, was of manageable size. He must have thought, a few weeks and I'll be at the far end. In fact, the fleet was to be at sea for almost four months.

As we saw, their provisions were almost gone when they entered the strait. How would they survive? Pigafetta writes:

Wednesday, November 28, 1520, we debouched from the strait, engulfing ourselves in the Pacific Sea. We were three months and twenty days without getting any kind of fresh food. We ate biscuit, which was no longer biscuit, but powder of biscuits swarming with worms, for they had eaten the good. It stank strongly of the urine of

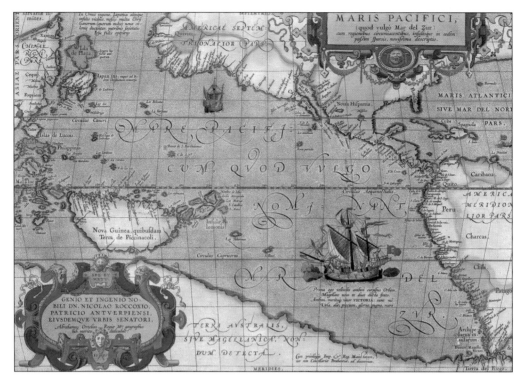

A map of the Pacific Ocean, from the atlas of 1570 created by Abraham Ortelius, the first modern geographer. It shows Magellan's ship the <u>Victoria</u>.

rats. We drank yellow water that had been putrid for many days. We also ate some ox hides that covered the top of the mainyard to prevent the yard from chafing the shrouds, and which had become exceedingly hard because of the sun, rain, and wind. We left them in the sea for four or five days, and then placed them for a few moments on top of the embers, and so ate them; and often we ate sawdust from boards. Rats were sold for one-half ducado apiece, and even then we could not get them. The gums of both the lower and upper teeth of some of our men swelled, so that they could not eat under any circumstances and therefore died.

Nineteen men died from that sickness.

SCURVY – THE SAILOR'S CURSE

With the poor diet of Magellan's men, the disease called scurvy was bound to occur. Many suffered terribly from it and a large number died. Symptoms included bleeding under the skin, around hair follicles, under the fingernails, around the gums, and into the joints. Victims became depressed, tired, and weak. Their blood pressure and heart rate fluctuated.

If the voyagers had been given blood tests, the results would have shown a very low level of vitamin C. That vitamin (ascorbic acid)—essential for the formation of the connective tissue that holds the body together—is found in citrus fruits, tomatoes, cabbage, and green peppers. When Magellan's men were able— by chance—to get the right food, they recovered, if they weren't too far gone.

Not until the eighteenth century did the need for antiscorbutics in seamen's rations come to be understood. Even then, skippers found it very hard to get sailors to eat their prescribed sauerkraut.

With singular bad luck Magellan's fleet managed to miss islands in the central Pacific where they could have found plenty of fresh food. But they were lucky in one respect: not once were they struck by storms. The Pacific Ocean, they felt, was rightly named.

Their first landfall, after long months, was at the Marianas. On March 6, 1521, they approached the island now known as Guam. When they dropped anchor, a swarm of outrigger canoes left the beach, and soon brown-skinned warriors were running over the deck of the *Trinidad*. They pillaged the ship of everything movable, ignoring the protests of the sick and feeble sailors. To get rid of them the crossbowmen fired a volley of arrows, killing several. The natives, terrified by weapons they had never seen before, scrambled off the ship and rowed ashore.

The next morning, Magellan, desperate for food and water, had all three ships bombard the seaside village. He then led forty armed men ashore, where they burned many of the thatched huts, killed seven people, and then gathered all the food left by the fleeing villagers—pigs, chickens, coconuts, bananas, rice, vegetables, and fruits. They filled water casks and then quickly put out to sea again.

At a nearby island Magellan traded for more food and again set sail. Better fed, the sailors who had been sick with scurvy began to recover. Magellan figured he must be very near the Moluccas. But no, these were not the Spice Islands, but the Philippines, as they would be later called after King Philip of Spain. On March 16, 1521, the fleet anchored at the big island of Homonhon. They were in Leyte Gulf, where four hundred years later the American navy would battle a Japanese fleet. When Magellan pitched tents on the beach to shelter scurvy victims, native people came to visit. They spoke no language Magellan's crew could understand. What the Europeans did understand was gold, and there was plenty to stare at—armlets and bracelets, even shields and weapons adorned with gold. Magellan cautioned his men to look indifferent, not greedy, or they would raise the bargaining price. He presented

A coconut tree.
To Magellan's
exhausted men,
coconuts were more
precious than gold.

the visitors with red caps, mirrors, combs, ivory, linen cloth, and other merchandise, while they gave him fresh fish, palm oil, bananas, and coconuts. Pigafetta noted that "all except the chief go naked," and that they were "dark, fat, and painted"—meaning tattooed.

The gold concerned Pigafetta far less than the coconuts. He soon learned what a treasure this strange fuzzy brown ball was. It provided food, wine, milk, oil, vinegar, and cordage, he noted, and when burned, the shell made an ash useful for medicine. For the crew sick with scurvy, coconut milk proved a godsend. The milk, plus oranges and fresh vegetables, speeded their recovery.

During a week's rest on the island, Magellan visited the sick men every day and served them the refreshing coconut milk. Then they sailed off again, and three days later stopped at the small island of Limasawa, off northern Mindanao. A friendly chief, Rajah Colambu, came aboard, whose language Enrique could understand. And he came with gold to trade. Magellan pretended only mild interest, and succeeded in setting the rate of exchange at one pound of gold for one pound of iron, a metal the islanders found far more useful.

On the flagship Colambu was given a demonstration of the value of European steel plate. Magellan had a sailor put on a suit of armor and had three others strike him repeatedly with swords and daggers. Seeing no injury done, the rajah was speechless. He invited Pigafetta and two officers to a royal luncheon at which they got drunk on palm wine.

On Easter Sunday Magellan took fifty men ashore to celebrate high Mass. A priest explained the ceremonies and the significance of the cross, nails, and crown of thorns that were brought in. The rajah kissed the cross, which pleased Magellan. That afternoon Magellan had a cross erected on the island's tallest peak and explained to the rajah that it would protect his people against any Christians who might later land there, as well as against lightning and storms. It was a sign of how intent Magellan had become on converting the natives he was now encountering.

It was time to move on. Colambu loaned the fleet pilots to take them to Cebu, an island he described as the richest in the archipelago. He offered to go along himself. But because it was time for the rice harvest, that must be completed first. Magellan assigned a company of sailors to help with the harvest.

On April 3, the fleet sailed out, and four days later it anchored in the harbor at Cebu. There, Rajah Humabon at first demanded tribute for permission to land. But told by a Siamese trader that people like these newcomers had conquered many places in India and Malacca, he changed his mind and reached a peaceful agreement with Magellan. He even allowed him to set up a shop on shore, and promised a hearty welcome to the crews. Hearty it was, for Pigafetta noted that "whenever any of our men went on shore, both by day and by night, everyone invited him to eat and drink." And he also bragged: "The women loved us very much more than their own men."

That displeased Magellan. He ordered his men to have nothing to do with any women unless they were baptized as Christians. Of course that made every sailor an ardent missionary.

To Christianize Cebu now became Magellan's burning desire. He told Humabon that adopting the new faith would enable him to conquer his enemies more easily. Some of Humabon's subordinates resisted the rajah's orders to convert. Magellan called them together and threatened to kill everyone who did not obey the rajah.

The fleet's priests raced to baptize the new converts. Pigafetta took pride in their accomplishment:

Counting men, women and children, we baptized 800 souls. Before that week had gone, all the persons of that island, and some from the other islands, were baptized. We burned one hamlet which was located in a neighboring island, because it refused to obey the king or us. We set up the cross there, for those people were heathen.

When Magellan grasped that many of the natives had multiple wives, he decided not to let that stop conversion. He must have thought that so long as the heathen burned their idols and accepted the cross, it was enough. Not only did he accept the islanders into the church, he had them all swear allegiance to the King of Spain. While bringing new souls to the kingdom of Christ, he would add new territory to the empire of Spain.

An artist's representation of Magellan's cross, in a ceiling painting in Cebu City, the Philippines.

The frenzy with which he went about this would bring death upon him. Word came that on the neighboring island of Mactan, the chief said he would have nothing to do with this Christianizing. Infuriated by his resistance, Magellan decided to make an example of him. He was confident there was little risk, for how could God let anyone interfere with his holy mission?

S E V E N

Death in the Islands

Shortly after midnight on April 27, 1521, Magellan, at the head of sixty armed volunteers, crossed the harbor to Mactan in long boats. Because of rocks in the water they could not reach the shore. When day broke Magellan and forty-eight of his men leaped into the water and waded almost half a mile to the beach. About 1,500 armed islanders were waiting for them. A fierce fight began, but the arrows and lances of the Mactan men were too much for Magellan's small force.

Seeing the invaders' legs were bare, the Mactan men shot low. A poisoned arrow struck Magellan's leg, and he ordered his men to withdraw slowly. But with a handful of faithful men, including Pigafetta, he stayed to cover their retreat. Pigafetta tells what happened next:

As a good captain and knight he still stood fast with some others,
fighting thus for more than an hour. And as he refused to retire

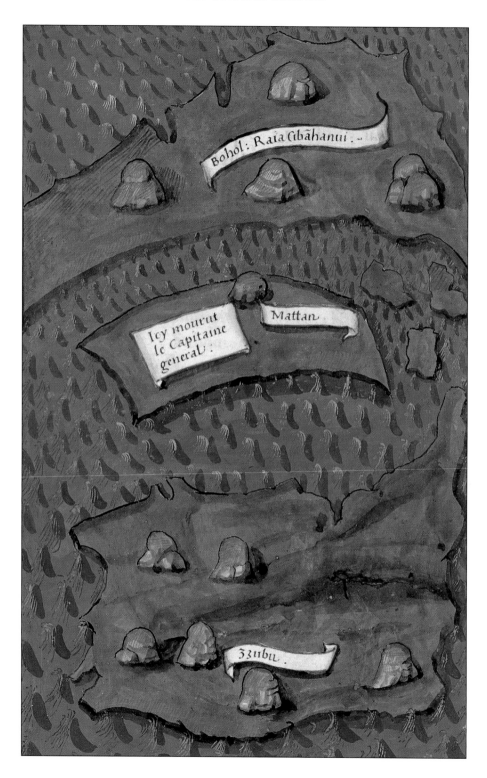

further, an Indian threw a bamboo lance in his face, and the captain immediately killed him with his lance. Then, trying to lay hand on his sword, he could draw it but half-way, because of a wound from a bamboo lance that he had in his arm. Which seeing, all those people threw themselves on him, and one of them with a large javelin thrust it into his left leg, whereby he fell face downward. On this all at once rushed upon with lances of iron and of bamboo and with these javelins, so that they slew our light, our comfort, and our true guide.

Too confident in the power of European weapons and too certain of God's protection, Magellan died. He did not personally complete the circumnavigation of the globe that he had begun in 1519. Yet it was his courage and determination that prevented the expedition from turning back. And in the end, a small remnant of his fleet would finish the task he had set himself.

With Magellan gone, the crew chose Duarte Barbosa, Magellan's brother-in-law, to be in command. Barbosa ordered Enrique, Magellan's slave and interpreter, himself wounded in the fight, to take a message to Rajah Humabon back on Cebu, asking him to assign native pilots for their continuing voyage. Enrique declined because of his wounds. Angered at the slave's refusal, Barbosa threatened to make sure Enrique would never be manumitted (freed), as Magellan's will had stipulated, but remain a slave for life. He ordered Enrique to get up or he would have him flogged.

So the furious Enrique went ashore. He returned with an invitation from Humabon for the top officers and ranking men to dine with him and receive gifts. The officers and some sixteen other men went gladly. When they were heavy with food and giddy with palm wine,

A map from Pigafatta's journal, showing, in the center, the island of Mactan, where Magellan died.

Humabon's men murdered or captured all but two of them. It seems that Humabon had decided to get rid of the Spaniards, abandon his new Christian faith, and return to his old gods.

The constable Espinosa and the pilot Carvalho escaped and rowed back to the fleet. Abandoned to their fate on Cebu were twenty-six men. They died soon after or were sold as slaves to China. No one knows what happened to Enrique.

Now Espinosa took command of the *Trinidad*, Carvalho of the *Victoria*, and Elcano of the *Concepcion*. They sailed to a nearby beach and reorganized. When they realized there were not enough men to man three ships, they scuttled the poorest—the *Concepcion*—and distributed its crew, gear, and cargo among the other two ships. Then they burned the *Concepcion*. Carvalho was elected captain of the *Trinidad* and Elcano of the *Victoria*.

Early in May the two ships set off on a southwesterly course. Throughout the summer and early autumn of 1521 they sailed almost randomly around islands of the Philippines and northern Indonesia. They seemed in no hurry to reach the Spice Islands. They were no longer finding new countries, but visiting communities with organized governments that had trading relations with China, Thailand, and India, and that the Portuguese too already knew. They traded with friendly people, some pagan, some Muslim.

On June 21 they docked at Brunei in northeastern Borneo. Its sultan greeted them handsomely, sent them gifts borne on elephants, and gave them permission to trade. But a week later the Spanish sailors, fearing a surprise assault by an approaching fleet of native boats, attacked first, killing several men and capturing four.

They then sailed to another island where they spent six weeks repairing the ships and laying in supplies. Under Magellan's leadership, strict discipline and a sense of mission had maintained morale. With their leader gone, the men behaved like pirates. Carvalho, who had all along been making personal deals with islanders, captured three Muslim women for his private harem. His arrogant behavior so offended the others that they put Espinosa in his place as captain of the *Trinidad*. The sailors, no saints themselves, kept pirating wherever they went, capturing native boats, killing some people, kidnapping others to guide them through the islands. Piracy at that time was a way of life in these waters. The sailors looked at the rich traffic between China and India as fair game.

On November 6 they at last found themselves in the Moluccas, the treasure house of products they hoped would make them all wealthy. They entered a port at Tidore, the most important of the spice islands.

Here they expected to meet Francisco Serrano, Magellan's old comrade-in-arms, who had long ago settled into a luxurious life on the

A beach in the Moluccas, with the Tidore volcano in the distance.

islands. Sadly, they learned that Serrano had died only eight months earlier, poisoned by a native prince who hated a Portuguese interfering in his politics. The historian Samuel Eliot Morison, who visited the Moluccas in the twentieth century, described the islands as "lofty and verdure-covered," but so tiny "that it is difficult to believe that in the sixteenth century they inspired momentous voyages, supported independent rulers in high state, and caused thousands of deaths among Europeans fighting to control their fragrant riches."

When they stopped on the shores of the Moro Gulf, Pigafetta recorded the cannibalism he said was practiced by a tribe on Mindanao: "Near a river are found shaggy men who are exceedingly great fighters and archers. They use swords one palmo in length, and eat only raw human hearts with the juice of oranges or lemons."

Pigafetta noted that each Moro prince had a principal wife and more than two hundred women in his harem. He told how clove trees were grown and the harvest gathered, and how sago, their bread, was prepared. The sultans made royal visits to the two ships and traded large amounts of cloves.

Cloves! Valuable cargo! To double their chances of reaching home with the spices, the officers decided that the *Victoria* should return by the Cape of Good Hope, while the *Trinidad* would await the westerly monsoon, then head for Spanish America, where the crew would carry the precious cargo across the Isthmus of Panama and ship it to Spain.

Cloves on a branch [inset] and drying in the sun. Magellan died before reaching Mindanao and its precious clove trees.

EIGHT

A Handful Return

The *Trinidad*, whose leaks were so bad they were hard to repair, delayed for three months before departing Tidore. She carried fifty tons of cloves when she sailed on April 6, 1521. On reaching the Mariana Islands, three men deserted. Captain Espinosa decided to return to Tidore. But during the six weeks it took the ship to stagger back, thirty of the crew of fifty-three died of scurvy, and the rest were so weakened that they barely made it.

On arrival, they found that a fleet of Portuguese warships on the hunt for Magellan had docked at Tidore and wiped out the small Spanish garrison stationed there. The Portuguese captured the *Trinidad*. Only five of the crew ever got back to Spain. Espinosa, whose steadfast support of Magellan in the San Julian mutiny had saved the expedition, spent more

In 1526, four years after Magellan's ship the <u>Victoria</u> completed its voyage, this globe was made, the earliest known map of the route. It was created in twelve sections, printed on paper, and mounted on a solid wooden ball. A vertical crack damaged it later.

than four years in captivity before he was allowed to return to Spain, where King Charles granted him a comfortable pension.

On the homeward voyage, the *Victoria* was captained by Elcano.

Ironically, he had been one of the chief mutineers at San Julian. His route to Spain was by way of the Cape of Good Hope—the only way to go, unless you were crazy enough to face Magellan's strait again. The ship left Tidore on December 21, 1521 with a crew of sixty, thirteen of them natives. They stopped once or twice for fresh provisions, and once for a week to caulk and repair the ship after storm damage. On January 25, 1522, they reached the mountainous island of Timor. Here, said Pigafetta, "White sandalwood is found, and nowhere else. Also, ginger, water buffaloes, swine, goats, fowls, rich figs [bananas], sugarcane, oranges, lemons, wax, almonds, kidney beans, and other things." The people were all heathens, he noted, and willing to trade. The ship coasted along the island for three weeks, trading for provisions.

Now they headed for the Cape of Good Hope, sailing straight across the Indian Ocean to avoid Portuguese patrols. It was agonizing, for they did not have enough food for so long a voyage. Lacking salt, their barreled meat and fish turned putrid. Head winds raised enormous seas, the *Victoria* could barely contend with. The ship was damaged and springing leaks. Its rigging was torn almost to tatters.

Some of the crew—cold, hungry, and sick—begged Elcano to risk capture and head for Portuguese Mozambique, which they mistakenly thought was close by. But the majority, said Pigafetta, "more desirous of honor than of their own life, determined to go to Spain living or dead." After several more weeks at sea, on May 8 they landed on the South African coast, thinking they were at the cape. But they were wrong. Finally they rounded the Cape and began sailing north, hunger and scurvy accompanying them all the way. On July 9 they reached the Cape Verde islands, which the Portuguese controlled. By this time twenty-one of the crew had died. Hunger, exhaustion, and disease had done them in.

Elcano hoped to buy food here as well as slaves to man the pumps. At first he deceived the Portuguese into believing the ship had simply lost its way returning from Spain's territories in the Caribbean. But when the thirteen men he sent ashore offered cloves in return for provisions and slaves, the Portuguese knew Elcano had been lying and sent armed men out to take the *Victoria* prisoner. Suspecting trouble, Elcano fled the harbor just in time, abandoning the thirteen men ashore.

This last leg of the voyage home was perhaps the hardest. There were only twenty-one men, many of them sick, to do the work of fifty. The ship had become so leaky they had to work the pumps day and night to keep from sinking. They passed by the Azores, unable to stop for repairs for fear of the Portuguese.

It was Monday, September 8, 1522, when the *Victoria* anchored

Taken from an Italian atlas of the sixteenth century, this map traces Magellan's circumnavigation of the globe.

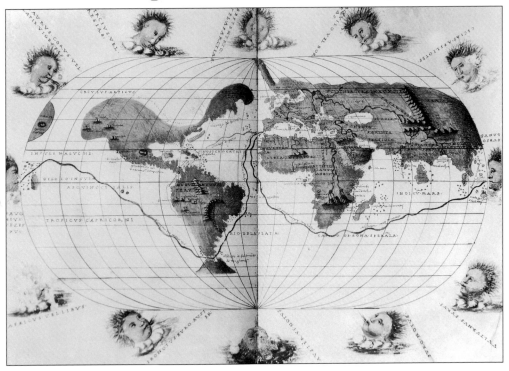

at Seville—three years and one month since she had sailed out of that harbor.

Twenty-one sickly survivors staggered ashore. The next day they went barefoot in their ragged shirts to the shrine of Santa Maria de la Victoria, to give thanks for their deliverance. Of the 270 men who sailed from Seville with Magellan in 1519, 35 eventually returned to Spain

King Charles congratulated Elcano and the crew on their great achievement, and honored them when they appeared at court. Pigafetta too was received by the king, to whom he presented "a book written by my hand of all the things that had occurred day by day on our voyage." That copy has been lost, but the French and Italian editions of his manuscript have survived.

NINE

An Immense Triumph

So ended the first circumnavigation of the globe. In one sense it had been a disaster. Three ships out of five had been lost. More than two hundred men had died or disappeared. And as a commercial enterprise? The *Victoria* brought back cloves, but their sale brought barely enough to cover the cost of the expedition.

Was the survivors' dream of getting rich fulfilled? No, for although Elcano received an annual pension from Charles, the others got little or nothing.

As for the conflicting claims to the Spice Islands, a conference between Spain and Portugal to determine which country had the right to trade and settle there came to nothing. Several years later, however, when Charles needed money, he gave up to Portugal all claims to the Moluccas in return for 350,000 gold ducats.

A sixteenth-century portrait of Magellan
by Italian artist Antonio Da Varese.

"It was a small return for so great an expenditure of lives, of persistence, of courage and of skill," said historian J. H. Parry. "Yet the most important cargo the Victoria brought back was not cloves, nor delusive commercial hopes, but information. The world, everyone knew, was round; in theory it was circumnavigable. Now it had been circumnavigated. In the course of circumnavigation, some well-entrenched beliefs . . . had to be abandoned, and major new facts to be accepted. The world turned out to be considerably larger than most people had supposed; a third great ocean, bigger than either of the others, stretched between Asia and the Americas . . . . The oceans of the world were all connected. Given skill and courage,

Coat-of-arms and signature of Magellan.

adequate stores and a reliable ship, a man could sail to any part of the world he wished."

If Magellan's exploit had occurred in modern times, the *Victoria* would have been preserved as a monument for all to gaze at reverently. Instead, she was repaired to make her seaworthy again, then sent out on a round-trip voyage to the West Indies. When she was sent a second time, she disappeared, with all hands lost.

Historians of the sea hold that Magellan's "was the greatest and most wonderful voyage in recorded history." But it would be many years before his name received the honor it deserves. The Portuguese denounced him as a traitor for taking service with Spain. And Elcano, a Spaniard who resented his Portuguese commander and had mutinied against him, repeated the lies told by the crew of the *San Antonio* to justify their desertion.

It was Pigafetta who did so much to make Europe realize the heroic achievement of Magellan. In the years following his return, he moved from court to court, telling eager listeners his thrilling, colorful stories of the long voyage.

Magellan's wife and two little children died before the *Victoria* reached Seville. The sole benefit to Magellan has been the fame accorded him now for centuries.

Magellan and His Times

1394: Prince Henry the Navigator is born

1433: Henry establishes his school for navigation

1460: Henry the Navigator dies

1470 to 1480: Ferdinand Magellan's birth (precise date unknown)

1488: Bartolomeu Dias rounds the Cape of Good Hope

1492: Columbus's first voyage

1494: Treaty of Tordesillas

1497 to 1498: Vasco de Gama rounds Cape of Good Hope and crosses Indian Ocean

1499: Amerigo Vespucci sails to South America

1500: Pedro Alvares Cabral discovers Brazil

1501: Vespucci sails to South America for Portugal

1505: Magellan's first voyage

1517: Magellan marries

1519: Magellan departs from Spain for the Spice Islands

1521: Magellan dies

FURTHER RESEARCH

Books

Jacobs, William J. *Magellan: Voyager with a Dream*. First Books, Watts, 1994

MacDonald, Fiona. *Magellan: A Voyage Around the World*. New York: Watts, New York, 1998

Meltzer, Milton. *Columbus and the World Around Him*. New York: Franklin Watts, 1990.

Steffof, Rebecca. *Ferdinand Magellan and the Discovery of the World Ocean*. World Explorers Series, Chelsea House, 1990.

Twist, Clint. *Magellan and DaGama*. Orlando, FL: Raintree Steck-Vaughn 1994

Websites

Explorers of the Millennium
http://tqjunior.advanced.org/403/magellan.html

The Mariner's Museum, Newport News, VA
http://www.mariner.org/age/magellan.html

BIBLIOGRAPHY

Boorstin, Daniel J. *The Discoverers.* New York: Vintage, 1985.

Braudel, Fernand. *Afterthoughts on Material Civilization and Capitalism.* Baltimore: Johns Hopkins Press, 1977.

Braudel, Fernand. *Capitalism and Material Life.* New York: Harper & Row, 1973.

Cameron, Ian. *Magellan and the First Circumnavigation of the World.* New York: Saturday Review Press, 1973.

Corn, Charles. *The Scents of Eden: A History of the Spice Trade.* New York: Kodansha, 1999.

Daniel, Hawthorne. *Ferdinand Magellan.* Garden City, NY: Doubleday, 1964.

Fritz, Jean. *Around the World in a Hundred Years: From Henry the Navigator to Magellan.* Putnam Publishing Group, 1998.

Hale, John R. *Age of Exploration.* New York: Time, 1966.

——. *Renaissance Europe: Individual and Society, 1480-1520.* Berkeley: University of California Press, 1977.

Jardine, Lisa. *Worldly Goods: A New History of the Renaissance.* New York: Nan A. Talese, 1996.

Joyner, Tim. *Magellan.* New York: McGraw-Hill, 1994

Knapton, Ernest John. *Europe: 1450-1815.* New York: Scribners, 1992.

Lopez, Robert S. *The Birth of Europe.* New York: M. Evans, 1967.

Meltzer, Milton. *Columbus and the World Around Him.* New York: Franklin Watts, 1990.

Morison, Samuel Eliot. *The Great Explorers: The European Discovery of America.* New York: Oxford University Press, 1978.

Parr, Charles McKew. *So Noble a Captain: The Life and Times of Ferdinand Magellan.* New York: Crowell, 1953.

Bibliography

Parry, J. H. *The Age of Reconaissance.* Berkeley: University of California Press, 1981.

——. *The Discovery of the Sea.* Berkeley: University of California Press, 1981.

Pigafetta, Antonio. *Magellan's Voyage: A Narrative of the First Circumnavigation.* New York: Dover, 1994.

Pirenne, Henri. *A History of Europe: Vol II: From the Thirteenth Century to the Renaissance and Reformation.* Garden City, NY: Doubleday Anchor Books, 1956.

Roditi, Edouard. *Magellan of the Pacific.* New York: McGraw-Hill Book Co., 1972.

Wolf, Eric R. *Europe and the People without History.* Berkeley: University of California Press, 1982.

Wright, Louis B. *Gold, Glory, and the Gospel: The Adventurous Lives and Times of the Renaissance Explorers.* New York: Atheneum, 1970.

INDEX

Index